WALKING

IN

Wisdom

A TOPICAL STUDY ON WISDOM
THROUGH THE BOOK OF PROVERBS

A LOVE GOD GREATLY JOURNAL

Contents

Welcome

WE ARE GLAD you have decided to join us in this Bible study! First of all, please know that you have been prayed for! It is not a coincidence you are participating in this study.

Our prayer for you is simple: that you will grow closer to our Lord as you dig into His Word each and every day! As you develop the discipline of being in God's Word on a daily basis, our prayer is that you will fall in love with Him even more as you spend time reading from the Bible.

Each day before you read the assigned scripture(s), pray and ask God to help you understand it. Invite Him to speak to you through His Word. Then listen. It's His job to speak to you, and it's your job to listen and obey.

Take time to read the verses over and over again. We are told in Proverbs to search and you will find: "Search for it like silver, and hunt for it like hidden treasure. Then you will understand" (Prov. 2:4–5 NCV).

We are thrilled to provide these different resources for you as you participate in our online Bible study:

- *Walking in Wisdom* Study Journal
- Reading Plan
- Weekly Blog Posts (Mondays, Wednesdays, and Fridays)
- Weekly Memory Verses
- Weekly Monday Videos
- Weekly Challenges
- Online Community: Facebook, Twitter, Instagram, LoveGodGreatly.com
- Hashtags: #LoveGodGreatly

All of us here at Love God Greatly can't wait for you to get started, and we hope to see you at the finish line. Endure, persevere, press on—and don't give up! Finish well what you are beginning today. We will be here every step of the way, cheering you on! We are in this together. Fight to rise early, to push back the stress of the day, to sit alone and spend time in God's Word! Let's see what God has in store for you in this study! Journey with us as we learn to love God greatly with our lives!

Our Community

LOVE GOD GREATLY (LGG) is a beautiful community of women who use a variety of technology platforms to keep each other accountable in God's Word.

We start with a simple Bible reading plan, but it doesn't stop there.

Some women gather in homes and churches locally, while others connect online with women across the globe. Whatever the method, we lovingly lock arms and unite for this purpose: to love God greatly with our lives.

In today's fast-paced technology-driven world, it would be easy to study God's Word in an isolated environment that lacks encouragement or support, but that isn't the intention here at Love God Greatly. God created us to live in community with Him and with those around us.

We need each other, and we live life better together.

Because of this, would you consider reaching out and doing this study with someone?

All of us have women in our lives who need friendship, accountability, and have the desire to dive into God's Word on a deeper level. Rest assured we'll be studying right alongside you—learning with you, cheering for you, enjoying sweet fellowship, and smiling from ear to ear as we watch God unite women together—intentionally connecting hearts and minds for His glory.

It's pretty unreal, this opportunity we have to grow not only closer to God through this study but also to each other. So here's the challenge: call your mom, your sister, your grandma, the girl across the street, or the college friend across the country. Gather a group of girls from your church or workplace, or meet in a coffee shop with friends you have always wished you knew better. Utilize the beauty of connecting online for inspiration and accountability, and take opportunities to meet in person when you can.

Arm-in-arm and hand-in-hand, let's do this thing…together.

How to SOAP

WE'RE PROUD OF YOU.

We really want you to know that.

We're proud of you for making the commitment to be in God's Word, to be reading it each day and applying it to your life, the beautiful life our Lord has given you.

In this study we offer you a study journal to accompany the verses we are reading. This journal is designed to help you interact with God's Word and learn to dig deeper, encouraging you to slow down and reflect on what God is saying to you that day.

At Love God Greatly, we use the SOAP Bible study method. Before beginning, let's take a moment to define this method and share why we recommend using it during your quiet time.

Why SOAP It?

It's one thing to simply read Scripture. But when you interact with it, intentionally slowing down to really reflect on it, suddenly words start popping off the page. The SOAP method allows you to dig deeper into Scripture and see more than you would if you simply read the verses and then went on your merry way. Please take the time to SOAP through our Bible studies and see for yourself how much more you get from your daily reading. You'll be amazed.

What Does SOAP Mean?

S stands for **Scripture**. Physically write out the verses. You'll be amazed at what God will reveal to you just by taking the time to slow down and write out what you are reading!

O stands for **observation**. What do you see in the verses that you're reading? Who is the intended audience? Is there a repetition of words? What words stand out to you?

A stands for **application**. This is when God's Word becomes personal. What is God saying to you today? How can you apply what you just read to your own personal life? What changes do you need to make? Is there action you need to take?

P stands for **prayer**. Pray God's Word back to Him. Spend time thanking Him. If He has revealed something to you during this time in His Word, pray about it. If He has revealed some sin that is in your life, confess. And remember, He loves you dearly.

Follow This Example

Scripture: Read and write out Colossians 1:5–8.

> "The faith and love that spring from the hope stored up for you in heaven and about which you have already heard in the true message of the gospel that has come to you. In the same way, the gospel is bearing fruit and growing throughout the whole world— just as it has been doing among you since the day you heard it and truly understood God's grace. You learned it from Epaphras, our dear fellow servant, who is a faithful minister of Christ on our behalf, and who also told us of your love in the Spirit" (NIV).

Observation: Write what stands out to you.

> When you combine faith and love, you get hope. We must remember that our hope is in heaven; it is yet to come. The gospel is the Word of truth. The gospel is continually bearing fruit and growing from the first day to the last. It just takes one person to change a whole community…Epaphras.

Application: Apply this scripture to your own life.

> God used one man, Epaphras, to change a whole town. I was reminded that we are simply called to tell others about Christ; it's God's job to spread the gospel, to grow it, and have it bear fruit. I felt today's verses were almost directly spoken to Love God Greatly women: "The gospel is bearing fruit and growing throughout the whole world—just as it has been doing among you since the day you heard it and truly understood God's grace."

It's so fun when God's Word comes alive and encourages us in our current situation! My passionate desire is that all the women involved in our LGG Bible study will understand God's grace and have a thirst for His Word. I was moved by this quote from my Bible commentary today: "God's Word is not just for our information, it is for our transformation."

Prayer: Pray over this.

> Dear Lord, please help me to be an "Epaphras," to tell others about You and then leave the results in Your loving hands. Please help me to understand and apply personally what I have read today to my life, thereby becoming more and more like You each and every day. Help me to live a life that bears the fruit of faith and love, anchoring my hope in heaven, not here on earth. Help me to remember that the best is yet to come!

SOAP It Up

Remember, the most important ingredients in the SOAP method are your interaction with God's Word and your application of His Word to your life:

> Blessed is the one who does not walk in step with the wicked or stand in the way that sinners take or sit in the company of mockers, but whose delight is in the law of the LORD, and who meditates on his law day and night. That person is like a tree planted by streams of water, which yields its fruit in season and whose leaf does not wither—whatever they do prospers. (Ps. 1:1–3, NIV)

Reading Plan

Week 1 - The Source of Wisdom

Monday	Read: Proverbs 1:1-7	SOAP: Proverbs 1:7
Tuesday	Read: Proverbs 2:1-6	SOAP: Proverbs 2:6
Wednesday	Read: Proverbs 3:5-8	SOAP: Proverbs 3:5-6
Thursday	Read: Proverbs 3:19-26	SOAP: Proverbs 3:19-20
Friday	Read: Proverbs 15:29-33	SOAP: Proverbs 15:33
Response Day		

Week 2 - Wisdom in Speech

Monday	Read: Proverbs 12:25; Proverbs 15:1-4	SOAP: Proverbs 15:1
Tuesday	Read: Proverbs 10:19; Proverbs 17:27-28; Proverbs 21:23	SOAP: Proverbs 10:19
Wednesday	Read: Proverbs 12:17-22	SOAP: Proverbs 12:22
Thursday	Read: Proverbs 25:11-15	SOAP: Proverbs 25:11
Friday	Read: Proverbs 31:25-26	SOAP: Proverbs 31:26
Response Day		

Week 3 - Wisdom in Relationships

Monday	Read: Proverbs 13:20; Proverbs 22:24-25	SOAP: Proverbs 13:20
Tuesday	Read: Proverbs 19:26; Proverbs 20:20; Proverbs 23:22	SOAP: Proverbs 23:22
Wednesday	Read: Proverbs 12:4; Proverbs 21:19; Proverbs 14:1	SOAP: Proverbs 14:1
Thursday	Read: Proverbs 3:12; Proverbs 22:6	SOAP: Proverbs 22:6
Friday	Read: Proverbs 24:17; Proverbs 25:21-22	SOAP: Proverbs 25:21
Response Day		

Week 4 - Wisdom in Work and Wealth

Monday	Read: Proverbs 13:4; Proverbs 24:30-34	SOAP: Proverbs 13:4
Tuesday	Read: Proverbs 11:18-20; Proverbs 20:17	SOAP: Proverbs 11:18
Wednesday	Read: Proverbs 3:9-10	SOAP: Proverbs 3:9
Thursday	Read: Proverbs 11:23-28	SOAP: Proverbs 11:25
Friday	Read: Proverbs 22:1-5	SOAP: Proverbs 22:1
Response Day		

Week 5 – Wisdom in Temptation

Monday	The Temptation of Unjust Gain	Read: Proverbs 1:10-19	SOAP: Proverbs 1:19
Tuesday	The Temptation of Excess	Read: Proverbs 20:1; Proverbs 23:19-21	SOAP: Proverbs 23:20
Wednesday	The Temptation of Adultery	Read: Proverbs 6:27-35	SOAP: Proverbs 6:32
Thursday	The Temptation of Evil	Read: Proverbs 4:20-27	SOAP: Proverbs 4:23
Friday	The Temptation to Withhold Good	Read: Proverbs 3:27-35	SOAP: Proverbs 3:27
Response Day			

Week 6 – The Fruit of Wisdom

Monday	Read: Proverbs 2:7-15	SOAP: Proverbs 2:7
Tuesday	Read: Proverbs 3:1-4	SOAP: Proverbs 3:4
Wednesday	Read: Proverbs 31:27-31	SOAP: Proverbs 31:30
Thursday	Read: Proverbs 8:10-21	SOAP: Proverbs 8:11
Friday	Read: Proverbs 24:3-6	SOAP: Proverbs 24:3-4
Response Day		

Goals

WE BELIEVE it's important to write out goals for this study. Take some time now and write three goals you would like to focus on as you begin to rise each day and dig into God's Word. Make sure and refer back to these goals throughout the next six weeks to help you stay focused. You can do it!

My goals are:

1.

2.

3.

Signature: _____

Date: _____

Introduction

YOU DON'T HAVE to live long to find out that life is full of choices, and that those choices have consequences. Some choices are as basic as deciding what we should eat for lunch, and other choices carry heavy commitments that can deeply affect our relationships, our work, our finances, and our futures. From the time we are infants until we've reached our final days on earth, each morning we wake up with two paths in front of us: the path of folly, and the path of wisdom.

The book of Proverbs positions us face-to-face with the wise and the fool and the consequences that follow them. A collection of pithy sayings primarily authored by King Solomon, this book is highly personal, at times uncomfortably transparent, and doesn't mess around in zeroing in on the world's greatest temptations that threaten to lead us astray from walking in the wisdom that God intended for us.

In this six-week study, you'll notice that our reading plan will guide us through a topical look at Proverbs, beginning in week one with the Source of wisdom. We'll then journey through no-nonsense proverbs that will point us to wisdom in our speech, our relationships, our work and wealth, and finally we'll discover how to apply wisdom in temptation. We'll wrap up our study looking at the fruit that results from walking in wisdom. Our prayer is that through this topical introduction you'll crave studying Proverbs in its entirety as a follow-up to our time together.

One important thing to keep in mind as we study is that proverbs are principles rather than promises. Promises are guaranteed, while principles focus on general truths. Parents who train their children in the way they should go (Proverbs 22:6) often witness the fruit of their children walking in the wisdom of the Lord as adults. However, because proverbs are not promises and we live in a fallen world, sometimes even the most diligent, faithful parents don't live in this reality.

As we prepare to begin, two well-known verses from the say-it-like-it-is book of Proverbs come to mind. While this book contains wisdom inspired by God that is applicable to nearly every imaginable area of life, the following verses sum up an even greater overarching purpose:

> Trust in the Lord with all your heart,
>
> and do not lean on your own understanding.
>
> In all your ways acknowledge him,
>
> and he will make straight your paths.
>
> Proverbs 3:5-6

Trust in the Lord instead of your own understanding: that is where the book of Proverbs ultimately leads us. God is the source of all wisdom, He uses these proverbs to show us the path that leads to wisdom, and He reveals to us the fruit of walking in this great wisdom… so that our trust is ultimately not in our floundering ways, but can be found securely in Him.

> "That your trust may be in the Lord,
>
> I have made them known to you today,
>
> even to you.
>
> Proverbs 22:19

Week 1

Week 1 Challenge (Note: You can find this listed in our Monday blog post):

Prayer focus for this week: Spend time praying for your family members.

	Praying	Praise
Monday		
Tuesday		
Wednesday		
Thursday		
Friday		

Trust in the Lord with all your heart,
and do not lean on your own understanding.
In all your ways acknowledge him,
and he will make straight your paths.

PROVERBS 3:5-6

Scripture for Week 1

THE SOURCE OF WISDOM

MONDAY *PROVERBS 1:1-7*

¹ The proverbs of Solomon, son of David, king of Israel:

² To know wisdom and instruction,
    to understand words of insight,
³ to receive instruction in wise dealing,
    in righteousness, justice, and equity;
⁴ to give prudence to the simple,
    knowledge and discretion to the youth—
⁵ Let the wise hear and increase in learning,
    and the one who understands obtain guidance,
⁶ to understand a proverb and a saying,
    the words of the wise and their riddles.
⁷ The fear of the Lord is the beginning of knowledge;
    fools despise wisdom and instruction.

TUESDAY *PROVERBS 2:1-6*

¹ My son, if you receive my words
    and treasure up my commandments with you,
² making your ear attentive to wisdom
    and inclining your heart to understanding;
³ yes, if you call out for insight
    and raise your voice for understanding,
⁴ if you seek it like silver
    and search for it as for hidden treasures,
⁵ then you will understand the fear of the Lord
    and find the knowledge of God.
⁶ For the Lord gives wisdom;
    from his mouth come knowledge and understanding;

WEDNESDAY *PROVERBS 3:5-8*

⁵ Trust in the Lord with all your heart,

and do not lean on your own understanding.
⁶ In all your ways acknowledge him,
and he will make straight your paths.
⁷ Be not wise in your own eyes;
fear the Lord, and turn away from evil.
⁸ It will be healing to your flesh
and refreshment to your bones.

THURSDAY   *PROVERBS 3:19-26*

¹⁹ The Lord by wisdom founded the earth;
by understanding he established the heavens;
²⁰ by his knowledge the deeps broke open,
and the clouds drop down the dew.
²¹ My son, do not lose sight of these—
keep sound wisdom and discretion,
²² and they will be life for your soul
and adornment for your neck.
²³ Then you will walk on your way securely,
and your foot will not stumble.
²⁴ If you lie down, you will not be afraid;
when you lie down, your sleep will be sweet.
²⁵ Do not be afraid of sudden terror
or of the ruin of the wicked, when it comes,
²⁶ for the Lord will be your confidence
and will keep your foot from being caught.

FRIDAY   *PROVERBS 15:29-33*

²⁹ The Lord is far from the wicked,
but he hears the prayer of the righteous.
³⁰ The light of the eyes rejoices the heart,
and good news refreshes the bones.
³¹ The ear that listens to life-giving reproof
will dwell among the wise.
³² Whoever ignores instruction despises himself,
but he who listens to reproof gains intelligence.
³³ The fear of the Lord is instruction in wisdom,
and humility comes before honor.

Monday

READ: Proverbs 1:1-7
SOAP: Proverbs 1:7

Scripture - Write out the **Scripture** passage for the day.

Observations - Write down 1 or 2 **observations** from the passage.

Monday

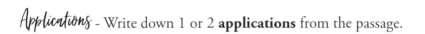

Applications - Write down 1 or 2 **applications** from the passage.

Pray - Write out a **prayer** over what you learned from today's passage.

-Visit our website today for the corresponding blog post!-

Tuesday

READ: Proverbs 2:1-6

SOAP: Proverbs 2:6

Scripture - Write out the **Scripture** passage for the day.

Observations - Write down 1 or 2 **observations** from the passage.

Tuesday

Applications - Write down 1 or 2 **applications** from the passage.

Pray - Write out a **prayer** over what you learned from today's passage.

Wednesday

READ: Proverbs 3:5-8
SOAP: Proverbs 3:5-6

Scripture - Write out the **Scripture** passage for the day.

Observations - Write down 1 or 2 **observations** from the passage.

Wednesday

Applications - Write down 1 or 2 **applications** from the passage.

Pray - Write out a **prayer** over what you learned from today's passage.

-Visit our website today for the corresponding blog post!-

Thursday

READ: Proverbs 3:19-26
SOAP: Proverbs 3:19-20

Scripture - Write out the **Scripture** passage for the day.

Observations - Write down 1 or 2 **observations** from the passage.

Thursday

Applications - Write down 1 or 2 **applications** from the passage.

Pray - Write out a **prayer** over what you learned from today's passage.

Friday

READ: Proverbs 15:29-33
SOAP: Proverbs 15:33

Scripture - Write out the **Scripture** passage for the day.

Observations - Write down 1 or 2 **observations** from the passage.

Friday

Applications - Write down 1 or 2 **applications** from the passage.

Pray - Write out a **prayer** over what you learned from today's passage.

-Visit our website today for the corresponding blog post!-

Reflection Questions

1. How is fearing the Lord linked to wisdom?

2. Who are we to turn to when we are seeking wisdom in our lives?

3. What are some ways that we gain wisdom?

4. Why is it important to acknowledge God in our lives?

5. How does your view of God affect your openness to receiving His wisdom?

My Response

Week 2

Week 2 Challenge (Note: You can find this listed in our Monday blog post):

Prayer focus for this week: Spend time praying for your country.

	Praying	Praise
Monday		
Tuesday		
Wednesday		
Thursday		
Friday		

She opens her mouth
with wisdom,
and the teaching of kindness
is on her tongue.

PROVERBS 31:26

Scripture for Week 2

WISDOM IN SPEECH

MONDAY *PROVERBS 12:25*

[25] Anxiety in a man's heart weighs him down,
   but a good word makes him glad.

PROVERBS 15:1-4

[1] A soft answer turns away wrath,
   but a harsh word stirs up anger.
[2] The tongue of the wise commends knowledge,
   but the mouths of fools pour out folly.
[3] The eyes of the Lord are in every place,
   keeping watch on the evil and the good.
[4] A gentle tongue is a tree of life,
   but perverseness in it breaks the spirit.

TUESDAY *PROVERBS 10:19*

[19] When words are many, transgression is not lacking,
   but whoever restrains his lips is prudent.

PROVERBS 17:27-28

[27] Whoever restrains his words has knowledge,
   and he who has a cool spirit is a man of understanding.
[28] Even a fool who keeps silent is considered wise;
   when he closes his lips, he is deemed intelligent.

PROVERBS 21:23

[23] Whoever keeps his mouth and his tongue
   keeps himself out of trouble.

WEDNESDAY PROVERBS 12:17-22

¹⁷ Whoever speaks the truth gives honest evidence,
   but a false witness utters deceit.
¹⁸ There is one whose rash words are like sword thrusts,
   but the tongue of the wise brings healing.
¹⁹ Truthful lips endure forever,
   but a lying tongue is but for a moment.
²⁰ Deceit is in the heart of those who devise evil,
   but those who plan peace have joy.
²¹ No ill befalls the righteous,
   but the wicked are filled with trouble.
²² Lying lips are an abomination to the Lord,
   but those who act faithfully are his delight.

THURSDAY PROVERBS 25:11-15

¹¹ A word fitly spoken
   is like apples of gold in a setting of silver.
¹² Like a gold ring or an ornament of gold
   is a wise reprover to a listening ear.
¹³ Like the cold of snow in the time of harvest
   is a faithful messenger to those who send him;
   he refreshes the soul of his masters.
¹⁴ Like clouds and wind without rain
   is a man who boasts of a gift he does not give.
¹⁵ With patience a ruler may be persuaded,
   and a soft tongue will break a bone.

FRIDAY PROVERBS 31:25-26

²⁵ Strength and dignity are her clothing,
   and she laughs at the time to come.
²⁶ She opens her mouth with wisdom,
   and the teaching of kindness is on her tongue.

Monday

READ: Proverbs 12:25; Proverbs 15:1-4
SOAP: Proverbs 15:1

Scripture - Write out the **Scripture** passage for the day.

Observations - Write down 1 or 2 **observations** from the passage.

Monday

Applications - Write down 1 or 2 **applications** from the passage.

Pray - Write out a **prayer** over what you learned from today's passage.

-Visit our website today for the corresponding blog post!-

Tuesday

READ: Proverbs 10:19; Proverbs 17:27-28; Proverbs 21:23

SOAP: Proverbs 10:19

Scripture - Write out the **Scripture** passage for the day.

Observations - Write down 1 or 2 **observations** from the passage.

Tuesday

Applications - Write down 1 or 2 **applications** from the passage.

Pray - Write out a **prayer** over what you learned from today's passage.

Wednesday

READ: Proverbs 12:17-22

SOAP: Proverbs 12:22

Scripture - Write out the **Scripture** passage for the day.

Observations - Write down 1 or 2 **observations** from the passage.

Wednesday

Applications - Write down 1 or 2 **applications** from the passage.

Pray - Write out a **prayer** over what you learned from today's passage.

-Visit our website today for the corresponding blog post!-

Thursday

READ: Proverbs 25:11-15

SOAP: Proverbs 25:11

Scripture - Write out the **Scripture** passage for the day.

Observations - Write down 1 or 2 **observations** from the passage.

Thursday

Applications - Write down 1 or 2 **applications** from the passage.

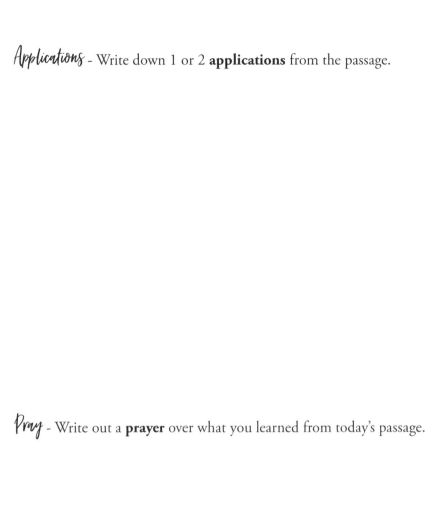

Pray - Write out a **prayer** over what you learned from today's passage.

Friday

READ: Proverbs 31:25-26
SOAP: Proverbs 31:26

Scripture - Write out the **Scripture** passage for the day.

Observations - Write down 1 or 2 **observations** from the passage.

Friday

Applications - Write down 1 or 2 **applications** from the passage.

Pray - Write out a **prayer** over what you learned from today's passage.

-Visit our website today for the corresponding blog post!-

Reflection Questions

1. How has someone else's words encouraged your heart just when you were needing it? What did they say?

2. The world tells us to "say it like it is," yet the Bible teaches us to restrain our words. Why is this important?

3. Reread Wednesday's verses. What is the result of a person's life who chooses to speak truth?

4. How are our words different when we choose to speak the truth in love?

5. Our words can be as valuable as jewels to those who receive them. Looking back over your week, how did you use your words? Did you build others up or tear them down?

My Response

Week 3

Week 3 Challenge (Note: You can find this listed in our Monday blog post):

Prayer focus for this week: Spend time praying for your friends.

	Praying	Praise
Monday		
Tuesday		
Wednesday		
Thursday		
Friday		

The wisest of women builds her house, but folly with her own hands tears it down.

PROVERBS 14:1

Scripture for Week 3

WISDOM IN RELATIONSHIPS

MONDAY *PROVERBS 13:20*

[20] Whoever walks with the wise becomes wise,

but the companion of fools will suffer harm.

PROVERBS 22:24-25

[24] Make no friendship with a man given to anger,

nor go with a wrathful man,

[25] lest you learn his ways

and entangle yourself in a snare.

TUESDAY *PROVERBS 19:26*

[26] He who does violence to his father and chases away his mother is a son who brings shame and reproach.

PROVERBS 20:20

[20] If one curses his father or his mother,

his lamp will be put out in utter darkness.

PROVERBS 23:22

[22] Listen to your father who gave you life, and do not despise your mother when she is old.

WEDNESDAY *PROVERBS 12:4*

[4] A worthy wife is a crown for her husband,

but a disgraceful woman is like cancer in his bones.

[19] It is better to live in a desert land than with a quarrelsome and fretful woman.

PROVERBS 14:1

[1] The wisest of women builds her house,
  but folly with her own hands tears it down.

THURSDAY   *PROVERBS 3:12*

[12] for the Lord reproves him whom he loves,
  as a father the son in whom he delights.

PROVERBS 22:6

[6] Train up a child in the way he should go;
  even when he is old he will not depart from it.

FRIDAY   *PROVERBS 24:17*

[17] Do not rejoice when your enemy falls,
  and let not your heart be glad when he stumbles,

PROVERBS 25:21-22

[21] If your enemy is hungry, give him bread to eat,
  and if he is thirsty, give him water to drink,
[22] for you will heap burning coals on his head,
  and the Lord will reward you.

Monday

READ: Proverbs 13:20; Proverbs 22:24-25
SOAP: Proverbs 13:20

Scripture – Write out the **Scripture** passage for the day.

Observations – Write down 1 or 2 **observations** from the passage.

Monday

Applications - Write down 1 or 2 **applications** from the passage.

Pray - Write out a **prayer** over what you learned from today's passage.

-Visit our website today for the corresponding blog post!-

Tuesday

READ: Proverbs 19:26 ; Proverbs 20:20; Proverbs 23:22

SOAP: Proverbs 23:22

Scripture - Write out the **Scripture** passage for the day.

Observations - Write down 1 or 2 **observations** from the passage.

Tuesday

Applications - Write down 1 or 2 **applications** from the passage.

Pray - Write out a **prayer** over what you learned from today's passage.

Wednesday

READ: Proverbs 12:4; Proverbs 21:19; Proverbs 14:1

SOAP: Proverbs 14:1

Scripture - Write out the **Scripture** passage for the day.

Observations - Write down 1 or 2 **observations** from the passage.

Wednesday

Applications - Write down 1 or 2 **applications** from the passage.

Pray - Write out a **prayer** over what you learned from today's passage.

-Visit our website today for the corresponding blog post!-

Thursday

READ: Proverbs 3:12; Proverbs 22:6
SOAP: Proverbs 22:6

Scripture - Write out the **Scripture** passage for the day.

Observations - Write down 1 or 2 **observations** from the passage.

Thursday

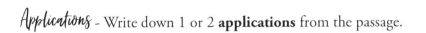

Applications - Write down 1 or 2 **applications** from the passage.

Pray - Write out a **prayer** over what you learned from today's passage.

Friday

READ: Proverbs 24:17; Proverbs 25:21-22
SOAP: Proverbs 25:21

Scripture - Write out the **Scripture** passage for the day.

Observations - Write down 1 or 2 **observations** from the passage.

Friday

Applications - Write down 1 or 2 **applications** from the passage.

Pray - Write out a **prayer** over what you learned from today's passage.

-Visit our website today for the corresponding blog post!-

Reflection Questions

1. How do you balance being a light in the world, yet choosing to walk with the wise?

2. What is the result of those who choose not to honor their parents?

3. Why is being selective in who your closest friends are important?

4. What are some ways that a woman can build up or tear her house apart?

5. Why do you think Jesus calls us to serve those who we consider our enemies? What benefit can it have to us?

My Response

Week 4

Week 4 Challenge (Note: You can find this listed in our Monday blog post):

Prayer focus for this week: Spend time praying for your church.

	Praying	Praise
Monday		
Tuesday		
Wednesday		
Thursday		
Friday		

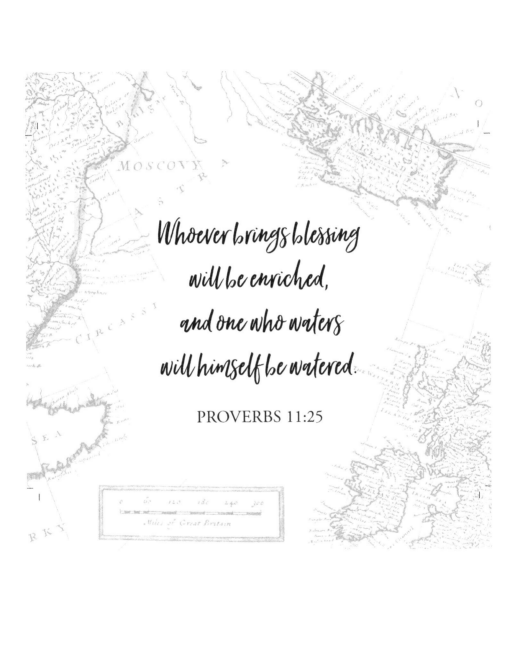

Whoever brings blessing
will be enriched,
and one who waters
will himself be watered.

PROVERBS 11:25

Scripture for Week 4

WISDOM IN WORK AND WEALTH

MONDAY *PROVERBS 13:4*

> ⁴ The soul of the sluggard craves and gets nothing,
>   while the soul of the diligent is richly supplied.

PROVERBS 24:30-34

> ³⁰ I passed by the field of a sluggard,
>   by the vineyard of a man lacking sense,
> ³¹ and behold, it was all overgrown with thorns;
>   the ground was covered with nettles,
>   and its stone wall was broken down.
> ³² Then I saw and considered it;
>   I looked and received instruction.
> ³³ A little sleep, a little slumber,
>   a little folding of the hands to rest,
> ³⁴ and poverty will come upon you like a robber,
>   and want like an armed man.

TUESDAY *PROVERBS 11:18-20*

> ¹⁸ The wicked earns deceptive wages,
>   but one who sows righteousness gets a sure reward.
> ¹⁹ Whoever is steadfast in righteousness will live,
>   but he who pursues evil will die.
> ²⁰ Those of crooked heart are an abomination to the Lord,
>   but those of blameless ways are his delight.

[17] Bread gained by deceit is sweet to a man,

but afterward his mouth will be full of gravel.

WEDNESDAY   *PROVERBS 3:9-10*

[9] Honor the Lord with your wealth

and with the first fruits of all your produce;

[10] then your barns will be filled with plenty,

and your vats will be bursting with wine.

THURSDAY   *PROVERBS 11:23-28*

[23] The desire of the righteous ends only in good,

the expectation of the wicked in wrath.

[24] One gives freely, yet grows all the richer;

another withholds what he should give, and only suffers
want.

[25] Whoever brings blessing will be enriched,

and one who waters will himself be watered.

[26] The people curse him who holds back grain,

but a blessing is on the head of him who sells it.

[27] Whoever diligently seeks good seeks favor,

but evil comes to him who searches for it.

[28] Whoever trusts in his riches will fall,

but the righteous will flourish like a green leaf.

FRIDAY   *PROVERBS 22:1-5*

[1] A good name is to be chosen rather than great riches,

and favor is better than silver or gold.

[2] The rich and the poor meet together;

the Lord is the Maker of them all.

³ The prudent sees danger and hides himself,
   but the simple go on and suffer for it.
⁴ The reward for humility and fear of the Lord
   is riches and honor and life.
⁵ Thorns and snares are in the way of the crooked;
   whoever guards his soul will keep far from them.

Monday

READ: Proverbs 13:4; Proverbs 24:30-34

SOAP: Proverbs 13:4

Scripture - Write out the **Scripture** passage for the day.

Observations - Write down 1 or 2 **observations** from the passage.

Monday

Applications - Write down 1 or 2 **applications** from the passage.

Pray - Write out a **prayer** over what you learned from today's passage.

-Visit our website today for the corresponding blog post!-

Tuesday

READ: Proverbs 11:18-20; Proverbs 20:17
SOAP: Proverbs 11:18

Scripture - Write out the **Scripture** passage for the day.

Observations - Write down 1 or 2 **observations** from the passage.

Tuesday

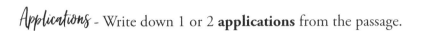

Applications - Write down 1 or 2 **applications** from the passage.

Pray - Write out a **prayer** over what you learned from today's passage.

Wednesday

READ: Proverbs 3:9-10
SOAP: Proverbs 3:9

Scripture - Write out the **Scripture** passage for the day.

Observations - Write down 1 or 2 **observations** from the passage.

Wednesday

Applications - Write down 1 or 2 **applications** from the passage.

Pray - Write out a **prayer** over what you learned from today's passage.

-Visit our website today for the corresponding blog post!-

Thursday

READ: Proverbs 11:23-28
SOAP: Proverbs 11:25

Scripture - Write out the **Scripture** passage for the day.

Observations - Write down 1 or 2 **observations** from the passage.

Thursday

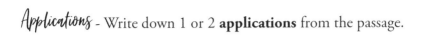

Applications - Write down 1 or 2 **applications** from the passage.

Pray - Write out a **prayer** over what you learned from today's passage.

Friday

READ: Proverbs 22:1-5
SOAP: Proverbs 22:1

Scripture - Write out the **Scripture** passage for the day.

Observations - Write down 1 or 2 **observations** from the passage.

Friday

Applications - Write down 1 or 2 **applications** from the passage.

Pray - Write out a **prayer** over what you learned from today's passage.

-Visit our website today for the corresponding blog post!-

Reflection Questions

1. Why do you think God made us to work? How does it help us in our everyday lives?

2. What is the consequence of ill-gotten wealth?

3. Why is it important to honor God with the wealth He has blessed us with in our lives?

4. Re-read Thursday's verses. What are some of the blessings for those who choose to be generous? What is the result of those who choose not to?

5. What are some ways you can be generous in your life? Remember, money is just one of many forms of generosity.

My Response

Week 5

Week 5 Challenge (Note: You can find this listed in our Monday blog post):

Prayer focus for this week: Spend time praying for missionaries.

Praying	Praise
Monday	
Tuesday	
Wednesday	
Thursday	
Friday	

Do not swerve to
the right or to the left;
turn your foot away from evil.

PROVERBS 4:27

Scripture for Week 5

WISDOM IN TEMPTATION

MONDAY – THE TEMPTATION OF UNJUST GAIN
PROVERBS 1:10-19

¹⁰ My son, if sinners entice you,

    do not consent.

¹¹ If they say, "Come with us, let us lie in wait for blood;

    let us ambush the innocent without reason;

¹² like Sheol let us swallow them alive,

    and whole, like those who go down to the pit;

¹³ we shall find all precious goods,

    we shall fill our houses with plunder;

¹⁴ throw in your lot among us;

    we will all have one purse"—

¹⁵ my son, do not walk in the way with them;

    hold back your foot from their paths,

¹⁶ for their feet run to evil,

    and they make haste to shed blood.

¹⁷ For in vain is a net spread

    in the sight of any bird,

¹⁸ but these men lie in wait for their own blood;

    they set an ambush for their own lives.

¹⁹ Such are the ways of everyone who is greedy for unjust gain;

    it takes away the life of its possessors.

TUESDAY – THE TEMPTATION OF EXCESS
PROVERBS 20:1

¹ Wine is a mocker, strong drink a brawler,

and whoever is led astray by it is not wise.

PROVERBS 23:19-21

¹⁹ Hear, my son, and be wise,

and direct your heart in the way.

²⁰ Be not among drunkards

or among gluttonous eaters of meat,

²¹ for the drunkard and the glutton will come to poverty,

and slumber will clothe them with rags.

WEDNESDAY – THE TEMPTATION OF ADULTERY
PROVERBS 6:27-35

²⁷ Can a man carry fire next to his chest

and his clothes not be burned?

²⁸ Or can one walk on hot coals

and his feet not be scorched?

²⁹ So is he who goes in to his neighbor's wife;

none who touches her will go unpunished.

³⁰ People do not despise a thief if he steals

to satisfy his appetite when he is hungry,

³¹ but if he is caught, he will pay sevenfold;

he will give all the goods of his house.

³² He who commits adultery lacks sense;

he who does it destroys himself.

³³ He will get wounds and dishonor,

and his disgrace will not be wiped away.

³⁴ For jealousy makes a man furious,

and he will not spare when he takes revenge.

³⁵ He will accept no compensation;

he will refuse though you multiply gifts.

THURSDAY – THE TEMPTATION OF EVIL
PROVERBS 4:20-27

²⁰ My son, be attentive to my words;

incline your ear to my sayings.

²¹ Let them not escape from your sight;

keep them within your heart.

²² For they are life to those who find them,

and healing to all their flesh.

²³ Keep your heart with all vigilance,

for from it flow the springs of life.

²⁴ Put away from you crooked speech,

and put devious talk far from you.

²⁵ Let your eyes look directly forward,

and your gaze be straight before you.

²⁶ Ponder the path of your feet;

then all your ways will be sure.

²⁷ Do not swerve to the right or to the left;

turn your foot away from evil.

FRIDAY – THE TEMPTATION TO WITHHOLD GOOD
PROVERBS 3:27-35

²⁷ Do not withhold good from those to whom it is due,

when it is in your power to do it.

²⁸ Do not say to your neighbor, "Go, and come again,

tomorrow I will give it"—when you have it with you.

²⁹ Do not plan evil against your neighbor,
who dwells trustingly beside you.

³⁰ Do not contend with a man for no reason,
when he has done you no harm.

³¹ Do not envy a man of violence
and do not choose any of his ways,

³² for the devious person is an abomination to the Lord,
but the upright are in his confidence.

³³ The Lord's curse is on the house of the wicked,
but he blesses the dwelling of the righteous.

³⁴ Toward the scorners he is scornful,
but to the humble he gives favor.

³⁵ The wise will inherit honor,
but fools get disgrace.

Monday

READ: Proverbs 1:10-19
SOAP: Proverbs 1:19

Scripture - Write out the **Scripture** passage for the day.

Observations - Write down 1 or 2 **observations** from the passage.

Monday

Applications - Write down 1 or 2 **applications** from the passage.

Pray - Write out a **prayer** over what you learned from today's passage.

-Visit our website today for the corresponding blog post!-

Tuesday

READ: Proverbs 20:1; Proverbs 23:19-21
SOAP: Proverbs 23:20

Scripture - Write out the **Scripture** passage for the day.

Observations - Write down 1 or 2 **observations** from the passage.

Tuesday

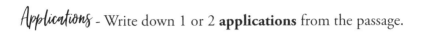

Applications - Write down 1 or 2 **applications** from the passage.

Pray - Write out a **prayer** over what you learned from today's passage.

Wednesday

READ: Proverbs 6:27-35
SOAP: Proverbs 6:32

Scripture - Write out the **Scripture** passage for the day.

Observations - Write down 1 or 2 **observations** from the passage.

Wednesday

Applications - Write down 1 or 2 **applications** from the passage.

Pray - Write out a **prayer** over what you learned from today's passage.

-Visit our website today for the corresponding blog post!-

Thursday

READ: Proverbs 4:20-27
SOAP: Proverbs 4:23

Scripture - Write out the **Scripture** passage for the day.

Observations - Write down 1 or 2 **observations** from the passage.

Thursday

Applications - Write down 1 or 2 **applications** from the passage.

Pray - Write out a **prayer** over what you learned from today's passage.

Friday

READ: Proverbs 3:27-35
SOAP: Proverbs 3:27

Scripture - Write out the **Scripture** passage for the day.

Observations - Write down 1 or 2 **observations** from the passage.

Friday

Applications - Write down 1 or 2 **applications** from the passage.

Pray - Write out a **prayer** over what you learned from today's passage.

-Visit our website today for the corresponding blog post!-

Reflection Questions

1. What should we teach our children about ill-gotten gain? What examples can you point to in our culture to show this Biblical consequence?

2. Without our desires in check, we always want more and more. How as Christians are we to deal with the temptations of excess?

3. If you are married, take a few moments and pray for your marriage and for protection from adultery. If you're not married, pray over your future marriage or the marriage of a friend or family member.

4. What we think about or look at tends to influence us. What are some ways you're guarding your eyes, your mind and instead focusing on Jesus?

5. Today, go and bless someone. Either bless them with your words, your time or your resources. Ask God to open your eyes to a need around you and then act on that need.

My Response

Week 6

Week 6 Challenge (Note: You can find this listed in our Monday blog post):

Prayer focus for this week: Spend time praying for you.

	Praying	Praise
Monday		
Tuesday		
Wednesday		
Thursday		
Friday		

for wisdom is better than jewels,
and all that you may desire cannot
compare with her.

PROVERBS 8:11

Scripture for Week 6

THE FRUIT OF WISDOM

MONDAY *PROVERBS 2:7-15*

⁷ he stores up sound wisdom for the upright;

he is a shield to those who walk in integrity,

⁸ guarding the paths of justice

and watching over the way of his saints.

⁹ Then you will understand righteousness and justice

and equity, every good path;

¹⁰ for wisdom will come into your heart,

and knowledge will be pleasant to your soul;

¹¹ discretion will watch over you,

understanding will guard you,

¹² delivering you from the way of evil,

from men of perverted speech,

¹³ who forsake the paths of uprightness

to walk in the ways of darkness,

¹⁴ who rejoice in doing evil

and delight in the perverseness of evil,

¹⁵ men whose paths are crooked,

and who are devious in their ways.

TUESDAY *PROVERBS 3:1-4*

¹ My son, do not forget my teaching,

but let your heart keep my commandments,

² for length of days and years of life

and peace they will add to you.

³ Let not steadfast love and faithfulness forsake you;

    bind them around your neck;

    write them on the tablet of your heart.

⁴ So you will find favor and good success

    in the sight of God and man.

WEDNESDAY   *PROVERBS 31:27-31*

²⁷ She looks well to the ways of her household

    and does not eat the bread of idleness.

²⁸ Her children rise up and call her blessed;

    her husband also, and he praises her:

²⁹ "Many women have done excellently,

    but you surpass them all."

³⁰ Charm is deceitful, and beauty is vain,

    but a woman who fears the Lord is to be praised.

³¹ Give her of the fruit of her hands,

    and let her works praise her in the gates.

THURSDAY   *PROVERBS 8:10-21*

¹⁰ Take my instruction instead of silver,

    and knowledge rather than choice gold,

¹¹ for wisdom is better than jewels,

    and all that you may desire cannot compare with her.

¹² "I, wisdom, dwell with prudence,

    and I find knowledge and discretion.

¹³ The fear of the Lord is hatred of evil.

Pride and arrogance and the way of evil

    and perverted speech I hate.

¹⁴ I have counsel and sound wisdom;

    I have insight; I have strength.

¹⁵ By me kings reign,

and rulers decree what is just;

¹⁶ by me princes rule,

and nobles, all who govern justly.

¹⁷ I love those who love me,

and those who seek me diligently find me.

¹⁸ Riches and honor are with me,

enduring wealth and righteousness.

¹⁹ My fruit is better than gold, even fine gold,

and my yield than choice silver.

²⁰ I walk in the way of righteousness,

in the paths of justice,

²¹ granting an inheritance to those who love me,

and filling their treasuries.

FRIDAY   *PROVERBS 24:3-6*

³ By wisdom a house is built,

and by understanding it is established;

⁴ by knowledge the rooms are filled

with all precious and pleasant riches.

⁵ A wise man is full of strength,

and a man of knowledge enhances his might,

⁶ for by wise guidance you can wage your war,

and in abundance of counselors there is victory.

Monday

READ: Proverbs 2:7-15
SOAP: Proverbs 2:7

Scripture - Write out the **Scripture** passage for the day.

Observations - Write down 1 or 2 **observations** from the passage.

Monday

Applications - Write down 1 or 2 **applications** from the passage.

Pray - Write out a **prayer** over what you learned from today's passage.

-Visit our website today for the corresponding blog post!-

Tuesday

READ: Proverbs 3:1-4
SOAP: Proverbs 3:4

Scripture - Write out the **Scripture** passage for the day.

Observations - Write down 1 or 2 **observations** from the passage.

Tuesday

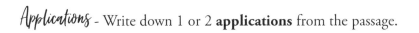

Applications - Write down 1 or 2 **applications** from the passage.

Pray - Write out a **prayer** over what you learned from today's passage.

Wednesday

READ: Proverbs 31:27-31
SOAP: Proverbs 31:30

Scripture - Write out the **Scripture** passage for the day.

Observations - Write down 1 or 2 **observations** from the passage.

Wednesday

Applications - Write down 1 or 2 **applications** from the passage.

Pray - Write out a **prayer** over what you learned from today's passage.

-Visit our website today for the corresponding blog post!-

READ: Proverbs 8:10-21
SOAP: Proverbs 8:11

Scripture - Write out the **Scripture** passage for the day.

Observations - Write down 1 or 2 **observations** from the passage.

Thursday

Applications - Write down 1 or 2 **applications** from the passage.

Pray - Write out a **prayer** over what you learned from today's passage.

Friday

READ: Proverbs 24:3-6
SOAP: Proverbs 24:3-4

Scripture - Write out the **Scripture** passage for the day.

Observations - Write down 1 or 2 **observations** from the passage.

Friday

Applications - Write down 1 or 2 **applications** from the passage.

Pray - Write out a **prayer** over what you learned from today's passage.

-Visit our website today for the corresponding blog post!-

Reflection Questions

1. Take a few moments and ask God for the wisdom you need right now in your life. We know from James 1:5 that God gives wisdom generously.

2. What are some ways you are seeking to gain wisdom in your life?

3. Beauty and charm don't last. What should we be investing our lives into? What gets better with age?

4. How does fearing the Lord help us grow in wisdom?

5. Who in your life are you seeking wisdom from?

My Response

Know these truths from God's Word...

God loves you.

Even when you're feeling unworthy and like the world is stacked against you, God loves you - *yes, you* - and He has created you for great purpose.

> God's Word says, "God so loved the world that He gave His one and only Son, Jesus, that whoever believes in Him shall not perish, but have eternal life" (John 3:16).

Our sin separates us from God.

We are all sinners by nature and by choice, and because of this we are separated from God, who is holy.

> God's Word says, "All have sinned and fall short of the glory of God" (Romans 3:23).

Jesus died so that you might have life.

The consequence of sin is death, but your story doesn't have to end there! God's free gift of salvation is available to us because Jesus took the penalty for our sin when He died on the cross.

> God's Word says, "For the wages of sin is death, but the free gift of

God is eternal life in Christ Jesus our Lord" (Romans 6:23); "God demonstrates His own love toward us, in that while we were yet sinners, Christ died for us" (Romans 5:8).

Jesus lives!

Death could not hold Him, and three days after His body was placed in the tomb Jesus rose again, defeating sin and death forever! He lives today in heaven and is preparing a place in eternity for all who believe in Him.

> God's Word says, "In my Father's house are many rooms. If it were not so, would I have told you that I go to prepare a place for you? And if I go and prepare a place for you, I will come again and will take you to myself, that where I am you may be also" (John 14:2-3).

Yes, you can KNOW that you are forgiven.

Accept Jesus as the only way to salvation…

Accepting Jesus as your Savior is not about what you can do, but rather about having faith in what Jesus has already done. It takes recognizing that you are a sinner, believing that Jesus died for your sins, and asking for forgiveness by placing your full trust in Jesus's work on the cross on your behalf.

> God's Word says, "If you confess with your mouth that Jesus is Lord and believe in your heart that God raised him from the dead, you will be saved. For with the heart one believes and is justified, and with the mouth one confesses and is saved" (Romans 10:9-10).

Practically, what does that look like? With a sincere heart, you can pray a simple prayer like this:

God,

I know that I am a sinner.

I don't want to live another day without embracing

the love and forgiveness that You have for me.

I ask for Your forgiveness.

I believe that You died for my sins and rose from the dead.

I surrender all that I am and ask You to be Lord of my life.

Help me to turn from my sin and follow You.

Teach me what it means to walk in freedom as I live under Your grace,

and help me to grow in Your ways as I seek to know You more.

Amen.

If you just prayed this prayer (or something similar in your own words), would you email us at info@lovegodgreatly.com? We'd love to help get you started on this exciting journey as a child of God!

a LoveGodGreatly Bible Study Journal

David

HIS STORY IS OUR STORY

Welcome, friend. We're so glad you're here...

LOVE GOD GREATLY exists to inspire, encourage, and equip women all over the world to make God's Word a priority in their lives.

-INSPIRE-	-ENCOURAGE-	-EQUIP-
women to make God's Word a priority in their daily lives through our Bible study resources.	women in their daily walks with God through online community and personal accountability.	women to grow in their faith, so that they can effectively reach others for Christ.

Love God Greatly consists of a beautiful community of women who use a variety of technology platforms to keep each other accountable in God's Word.

We start with a simple Bible reading plan, but it doesn't stop there.

Some gather in homes and churches locally, while others connect online with women across the globe. Whatever the method, we lovingly lock arms and unite for this purpose...

to Love God Greatly with our lives.

At *Love God Greatly*, you'll find real, authentic women. Women who are imperfect, yet forgiven. Women who desire less of us, and a whole lot more of Jesus. Women who long to know God through his Word, because we know that Truth transforms and sets us free. ***Women who are better together, saturated in God's Word and in community with one another.***

Love God Greatly is a 501 (C) (3) non-profit organization. Funding for Love God Greatly comes through donations and proceeds from our online Bible study journals and books. LGG is committed to providing quality Bible study materials and believes finances should never get in the way of a woman being able to participate in one of our studies. All LGG journals and translated journals are available to download for free from LoveGodGreatly.com for those who cannot afford to purchase them. Our journals and books are also available for sale on Amazon. Search for "Love God Greatly" to see all of our Bible study journals and books. 100% of proceeds go directly back into supporting Love God Greatly and helping us inspire, encourage and equip women all over the world with God's Word.

THANK YOU for partnering with us!

What we offer:

18 + Translations | Bible Reading Plans | Online Bible Study
Love God Greatly App | 80 + Countries Served
Bible Study Journals & Books | Community Groups

Each Love God Greatly study includes:

Three Devotional Corresponding Blog Posts | Monday Vlog Videos
Memory Verses | Weekly Challenge | Weekly Reading Plan
Reflection Questions And More!

Other Love God Greatly studies include:

David | Ecclesiastes | Growing Through Prayer | Names Of God
Galatians | Psalm 119 | 1st & 2nd Peter | Made For Community | Esther
The Road To Christmas | The Source Of Gratitude | You Are Loved

YOU CAN FIND US ONLINE AT LOVEGODGREATLY.COM

Made in the USA
Monee, IL
30 October 2021